D0757665

AMAZING INVENTIONS

AUTOMOBILE

MARY ELIZABETH SALZMANN

Consulting Editor, Diane Craig, M.A./Reading Specialist

Sandcastle

An Imprint of Abdo Publishing
abdopublishing.com

abdopublishing.com

Published by Abdo Publishing, a division of ABDO, PO Box 398166, Minneapolis, Minnesota 55439. Copyright © 2016 by Abdo Consulting Group, Inc. International copyrights reserved in all countries. No part of this book may be reproduced in any form without written permission from the publisher. SandCastle™ is a trademark and logo of Abdo Publishing.

Printed in the United States of America, North Mankato, Minnesota

062015
092015

Editor: Alex Kuskowski
Content Developer: Nancy Tuminelly
Cover and Interior Design and Production: Mighty Media, Inc.
Photo Credits: City of Vancouver BC, Library of Congress, Shutterstock, Wikimedia

Library of Congress Cataloging-in-Publication Data

Salzmann, Mary Elizabeth, 1968- author.
  Automobile / Mary Elizabeth Salzmann ; consulting editor, Diane Craig, M.A./Reading Specialist.
    pages cm. -- (Amazing inventions)
  Audience: Grades PreK-3.
  ISBN 978-1-62403-708-5
1. Automobiles--Juvenile literature. 2. Inventions--History--Juvenile literature. I. Title.
TL147.S25 2016
  629.222--dc23
                    2014045325

SandCastle™ Level: Fluent

SandCastle™ books are created by a team of professional educators, reading specialists, and content developers around five essential components—phonemic awareness, phonics, vocabulary, text comprehension, and fluency—to assist young readers as they develop reading skills and strategies and increase their general knowledge. All books are written, reviewed, and leveled for guided reading, early reading intervention, and Accelerated Reader™ programs for use in shared, guided, and independent reading and writing activities to support a balanced approach to literacy instruction. The SandCastle™ series has four levels that correspond to early literacy development. The levels are provided to help teachers and parents select appropriate books for young readers.

EMERGING · BEGINNING · TRANSITIONAL · FLUENT

CONTENTS

ALL ABOUT
AUTOMOBILES

There are many kinds of automobiles.
An automobile is a car.

Cars **replaced** the horse and **buggy**.

People called early cars horseless **carriages**.

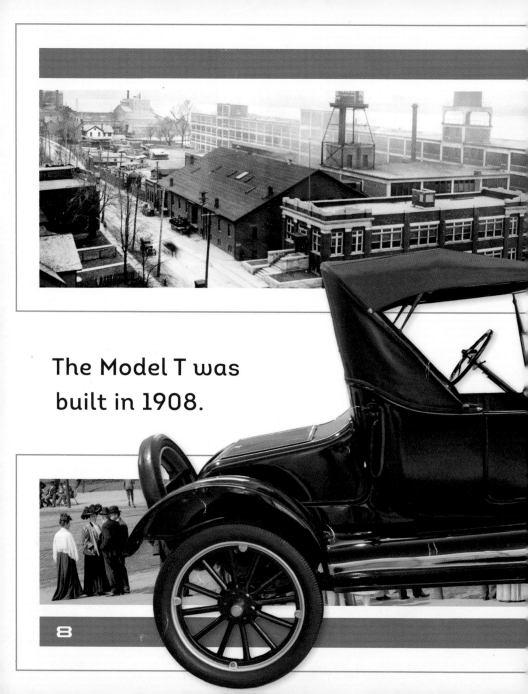

The Model T was built in 1908.

It was the first popular car. Most people could afford to buy it.

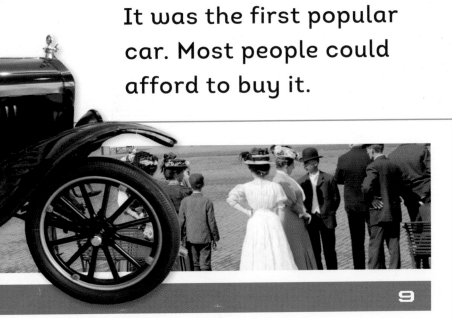

The first cars had **cranks**.
Turning the crank
started the car.

Now people
turn a key.

Gas is the most common **fuel** for cars.
Gas is burned in the car's engine.

Some cars run on electricity. They get **plugged in** to **recharge**.

Cars are made in factories. The factories have **assembly** lines.

Cars didn't always have seat belts.
They became standard in the 1960s.

Jenny always uses her seat belt.

A car might stop working.

José helps his dad fix their car.

THINK ABOUT IT

What kind of car would you like to ride in? Where would you go?

GLOSSARY

assemble – to put something with many parts together.

buggy – a cart for people to ride in that is pulled by one horse.

carriage – a vehicle pulled by horses that people ride in.

crank – a handle that is turned to start or run a machine.

fuel – a material used to power machines.

plug in – to attach to a source of electricity.

recharge – to refill a battery with stored electrical energy.

replace – to put something new in the place of.